Growing up with the
NORTH AMERICAN
INDIANS

Pat Hodgson

Batsford Academic and Educational Limited London

ISBN 0 7134 2732 9

Printed in Hong Kong
for the Publishers Batsford Academic and
Educational Limited,
4 Fitzhardinge Street, London W1H 0AH

Frontispiece: **A Chippewa girl**

Acknowledgment

The Author and Publishers thank the following for
their kind permission to reproduce copyright
illustrations: BBC Hulton Picture Library for figs 1,
2, 3, 7, 22, 26, 27, 31, 35, 45, 53, 61, 62; the
Trustees of the British Museum for figs 14, 32, 47,
48; Dover Publications Ltd for figs 9, 10, 23, 40;
Exeter Museums Service for fig 30; Exeter University
Library for figs 11, 20, 63; Pat Hodgson Library for
figs 8, 24, 25, 28, 34, 38, 43, 44, 50, 60; The
Horniman Museum for figs 12, 33, 56; Museum of
the American Indian Heye Foundation for fig 18;
New York State Museum and Science Service for
fig 17; Peter Newark's Western Americana for figs
5, 6, 15, 16, 21, 36, 37, 39, 41, 42, 46, 49, 51, 52,
54, 55, 57, 58, 59; Smithsonian Institution, National
Anthropological Archives for figs 13, 19, 29. The
map, fig 4, was drawn by Mr R. Britto.

Contents

The Illustrations

1 Introduction

When the first explorers from Europe came to America in the early sixteenth century, they were frightened and awed by the people they found there. The native Indians were quite unlike anyone that the Europeans has seen before. Many of the first Spanish and English explorers were soldiers looking for wealth, in particular gold, for themselves and their country. They met Indians whose way of life resembled that followed in Europe some one thousand years earlier. Many of the Indians were hunters with no settled homes. They had no towns, transport, industry, metal or firearms and no

1　Early explorers to America were amazed at the "stone age" way of life of the American Indians. This is a drawing by John White, to illustrate Sir Walter Raleigh's expedition to Virginia and Florida, 1585-1590.

2 A typical Indian face.

written language or schooling. Tools were primitive and made of stone. Only in Mexico and Peru had Indian civilizations developed which could be compared with those of the "Old World". It was easy for the explorers, who were afraid of these strange men, to try to overcome that fear by despising them for being backward. Present-day Americans have never forgotten their forefathers' wonder, when they met for the first time the mysterious and often hostile Indians. Stories about "Red Indians" are part of American folklore, but very little attempt was made to understand the Indian culture until it was too late. The "stone age" way of life followed by the Indians could not stand up to the influence of immigrants from the Old World, who energetically pushed westward into the "New

6

World" during the next three hundred years, overrunning Indian territory.

The tribes

Although all American Indians look similar and have common customs, in fact there were numerous different tribes living in the country when the first explorers arrived. If the explorers had not come for another four hundred years, these tribes might have banded together, made alliances, drawn up frontiers and become nations like the different countries of Europe. But there was no possibility of such gradual evolution once Indians came into contact with the doubtful benefits of Old World civilization.

American Indians are descendants of Mongols from Siberia, who crossed into the far north in prehistoric times, when the frozen Bering Straits joined the American continent to Europe. Most Indians have wide faces, with prominent cheek-bones and a yellowish skin, tanned by the sun to a brown or reddish colour, giving them the nickname "Redskins". Their hair is black and straight and they have little or no hair on their faces or bodies. Columbus first named them "Indians" when he landed at San Salvador in 1492, but thought he had arrived in India.

The Red Indians of Western films are based on Plains Indians of the mid-nineteenth century. Their way of life was that of only a small number of tribes at a particular stage in their history. Before white explorers

3   A drawing of Columbus's expedition to the "New World", showing the different methods the Indians had invented for crossing a river. Before the Europeans arrived, the Indians had no transport at all.

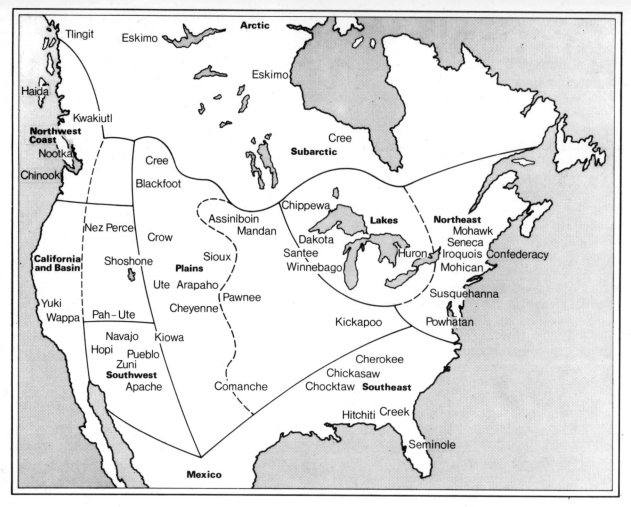

4   The territories of the major tribes.

arrived, native Indians had no transport at all. They had to walk everywhere, with only dogs to help carry their possessions. Isolated communities grew up all over America, each one with its own customs, language and culture, and having little contact with its neighbours. The kind of life that an Indian led depended on the climate and natural resources of his territory. In the far north of the continent Eskimos lived in igloos and hunted seal, whale, bear and caribou. In Central and South America there were the great Indian civilizations of Mexico and Peru, which were destroyed by Spanish invaders. Between these two extremes lived many various North American tribes. The more settled communities were generally in the south, towards the Mexican border. In the South West, the area now Arizona and New Mexico, the Pueblo, Hopi, Zuni and Navajo were farmers and tended to live in permanent homes so that they could cultivate their fields. The Pueblo had quite large houses made from mud brick and stone, and enough spare time to make pottery, rugs and jewellery of great beauty. On the other hand, the Pah-Utes, Wappa and Yuki in the neighbouring territory of California had a job to keep alive at all in the desert. They existed on wild plants and roots, and were despised by other tribes. Only communities living beside the sea had a regular supply of food near at hand. Climate and conditions were also easier for tribes like the Shoshone and Nez Perce, who lived in the high plateau country north of California, now Idaho, Oregon and East Montana.

On the North West Pacific Coast, between northern California and Alaska, early explorers found a distinctive and advanced Indian culture quite different from any other, The Chinook, Nootka and Haida lived in an isolated forest area rather like parts of Norway, where the rivers were full of salmon. There was plenty of wood for building houses, and abundant food, giving these Indians leisure to develop elaborate customs, religious rituals and an exotic art. When Captain Cook landed there in 1778, he noticed that the Indians wore curious masks, carved with the heads of birds and animals. He thought that travellers less sophisticated than he might well imagine that they had found a new "race of beings, partaking of the nature of man and beast".

The eastern side of North America, from Canada and the Great Lakes in the north down to Florida in the south, was a pleasant, fertile, woodland area, where the Indians cultivated maize and hunted game. The Dakotas and Assiniboins lived in the coniferous forests of the north. Going south, the coniferous trees gradually gave way to elm, birch and pine. This was the territory of the Iroquoians, Mohawks and Susquehanna. The mangrove swamps and wild rice fields of Florida were Cherokee, Creek and Seminole country.

The Great Plains run through the centre of the North American continent, from the Rocky Mountains in the north to the Rio

5   Zuni Indians planting corn, using the traditional digging stick.

Grande in western Texas. Although it is this part of America which is the background to Hollywood Westerns, early explorers found settled farming communities here, where the men hunted on foot. It was only when horses were introduced into the country by white explorers that the Plains Indians gave up agriculture for a more nomadic, hunting existence. Among the great tribes of the Plains area were the Blackfoot and Crow in Montana, the Mandan and Sioux of Dakota, the Pawnee of Nebraska and the Cheyenne of Colorado and Wyoming. The far south was Comanche and Apache territory.

An Indian child at the time of the first explorers would have had much in common with members of another tribe of the same age group, but, like a French boy compared with a Greek in Europe today, his language and habits might be different. The village encompassed a child's world. He would be taught to recognize friendly and hostile tribes, but would see little of any outsider, except perhaps at special celebrations. He would only go beyond the village when he had learnt how to survive in the wild alone.

The first settlers
American Indians first learnt to fear white men when Spanish soldiers, led by Cortes in Mexico and by Pizarro in Peru, destroyed the complex civilizations of the Aztecs and Incas in the early sixteenth century. At about the same date a more peacefully inclined French expedition, under Jacques

6   Nez Perce Indians outside their tepee, with a dog travois, 1870s.

7 One of John White's drawings of an exotic ► Indian.

Cartier, was exploring Canada. Sir Walter Raleigh sent the first English settlers to Virginia in 1585. A second expedition in 1587 was led by John White, who became fascinated with Indian life and brought back drawings of the people, plants and animals, which he hoped might attract more settlers. White found the Indians "gentle, loving and faithful, lacking all guile and trickery. . . as if they lived in a golden age". However, both parties of English settlers vanished without trace. More English colonists set sail again in 1606 for Virginia, and founded Jamestown. This time their leader, John Smith, was captured by the Algonquian chief Powhaton, and would have been killed but for the intervention of the chief's daughter, Pocohontas. Pocohontas later married a colonist, Thomas Rolfe, and went to live in England. In 1620 the Pilgrim Fathers landed in New England and further south, Quakers under William Penn founded Pennsylvania. Attempts were made to convert neighbouring Indian tribes to Christianity.

As time went by, settlers pushed their way deeper into the country. In the eighteenth century wars with the French and the American War of Independence drew Indians into white men's quarrels. Needing more land, in 1803 the United States Government purchased Louisiana from France. Soon afterwards, in 1830, the Removal Bill forced tribes living in the Louisiana area to leave their homes and move westward. Indian life was changing fast, and in 1832 a young American called George Catlin decided to live among the Plains Indians so that he could record "a dying nation, who have no historians or biographers of their own" before it was too late. The Plains Indians whom Catlin painted and described in his diaries, had based their entire way of life on the use of horses, which had only been introduced into the country comparatively recently by Spanish soldiers. Tools and guns, which they had obtained through trade with white settlers, were also making their lives easier. They had not much more than one hundred years of their new prosperity. By the 1880s their economy had been completely destroyed, many of their people had been killed and their leaders imprisoned. It is through

11

Catlin's eyes that we see what it was like to be an Indian in North America one hundred and fifty years ago, before the old life had been destroyed for ever.

8   An illustration from Captain John Smith's book *Virginia,* showing his being taken prisoner and strapped to a tree to be shot to death, 1606. But he was saved by the Indian chief's daughter.

C. Smith bound to a tree to be shott to death 1607

2 The Spirit World

The spirit world was as real to a young American Indian as the everyday scenes around him. Indians have never divided life into separate categories as we do. They thought of the world as a harmonious whole, with men, animals and spirits having equal positions in it. The earth was bountiful and belonged to everyone. As Luther Standing Bear wrote:

> We did not think of the great open plains, the beautiful rolling hills, and winding streams with tangled growth as 'wild'. Only to the white man was nature a 'wilderness' and only to him was the land 'infested' with 'wild' animals and 'savage' people. To us it was tame. Earth was bountiful and we were surrounded with the blessings of the Great Mystery. (*Land of the Spotted Eagle*, 1933).

Ghosts and spirits lurked in the forests and in the fields. They were in the flowers, the crops and the trees. They also inhabited the sky and the stars. They were ever-present in animals, who watched over men. Indian children took the spirit world for granted, although they were often frightened by some of its aspects. In recent times an Indian called Sounding Voice told Arthur Parker:

> Everything understands — bees, bugs, katydids, snakes and even coons. They are all what you might call brothers —

9 A mid-19th-century Iroquois illustration entitled "Returning Thanks to the Great Spirit". The Great Spirit was one of the three main deities worshipped by the Indians.

10 A drawing of an Eskimo mythic creature, ►
which was believed to be visible only to shamans.

the same Great Spirit made them all
out of the same thing. That's why everything understands, even dust. (Arthur
Parker, *The Indian How Book*, 1927).

Indian mythology

As there was no written language until the
late nineteenth century, Indian children
learnt about religion from their parents
or from tribal storytellers. These were
people with good memories who were
trained to recite legends so that they should
not be forgotten. Children really believed
the stories they were told about gods and
spirits. The tales were much more than
fairy stories. They were the tribe's religion,
history and literature. They provided ex-
planations of natural phenomena like the
stars, the weather and the creatures of
the world. Legends of a tribe were also
perpetuated by means of paintings and in
dancing and songs at the various festivals
during the year.

Although every tribe had its own particular legends, the stories had much in common. Differences in detail were due to the
contrasting areas in which people lived.
The dark, mysterious woods inhabited by
the Iroquois and other forest Indians encouraged them to imagine ghosts and spirits,
giants and dwarfs. An ice giant named
Windigo roamed the northern forests,
eating unwary travellers. Many of the
forest Indians' myths were about animals.
A terrible panther lived under water in the
Great Lakes area, dragging people from the
shore, down to its watery home. On the
other hand, tribes like the Seminole, who
were farmers, told stories about the spirits
of corn, rain and sun, who made the crops
grow. In a Seneca legend the corn goddess
reveals herself first to an old woman, saying:
"You and your people must care for me.
You must not permit weeds to kill me.

You shall see me sprout and grow to matur-
ity; and it is a truth that in the future all
the people who shall be born will see that I
will provide for their welfare . . . . I am
sweet corn. I am the first corn that came or
was delivered to this earth."

Indians believed in many gods, not one.
The three main deities, common to all
tribes but with many different names, were
the Great Spirit, the Earth Mother and the
Trickster. The Great Spirit was worshipped
more as an elemental force than as a personal
god, although George Catlin noted in his
diary that the Mandan Indians had a festival
devoted to the Great Spirit each year where
everyone could be seen "denying and
humbling themselves before him". The
Earth Mother was worshipped as the corn
goddess by farming tribes. A Tewa chant
went:

Oh, our Mother, the Earth; oh, our
Father the Sky
Your children are we, and with tired backs
We bring you the gifts that you love.

The Trickster was a curious god, particularly
popular among Plains Indians. He appeared
in animal or human form and could perform
heroic deeds as well as play practical jokes,
sometimes of a cruel nature. The Hitchiti
believed that the Trickster in rabbit form

14

discovered fire for the world. The Crow visualized the god as a coyote. He appeared to the Blackfoot as Napiw, an old man. Children loved to hear stories about the Trickster's pranks.

All tribes had legends about the creation of the world. The Iroquois believed that men had once lived in the sky. Beneath them there was only sea. One day a girl fell out of the sky into the water, and she was saved from drowning by a helpful toad, who spat out some earth onto a turtle's back for her to live on. This earth grew into the land we know, which is still supported on a turtle's back. Another common belief was that there had been a great flood in antiquity. An Eskimo legend describes how there were no animals before the earth was flooded. As the waters went down, a group of people made a journey by boat. Because the boat was too full, they threw a woman passenger overboard, and then chopped off her fingers, to stop her hanging on to the side. Her mutilated fingers grew miraculously into seals, walrus, whales and white bears, but bears still hate human beings for the way they treated the woman.

The Medicine Man
Although anyone could ask gods and spirits for favours, a Medicine Man was the magical expert of a tribe. He was priest, conjuror, visionary, doctor and leader. Children quickly learnt to respect and fear him. George Catlin gives a good definition of the word "Medicine" in his diary:

'Medicine' is a great word in this country . . . the word 'Medicine', in its common acceptation here, means *mystery*, and nothing else.

Other names for a Medicine Man are "shaman" or "witch doctor". A boy who found he was able to have visions might be trained to become a Medicine Man. Girls did not have this opportunity, although some older, married women sometimes had visions and cured sickness. The job of Medicine Man was not necessarily a secure one, as a shaman could be dismissed if his visions ceased or his magic was unsuccessful. Medicine Men charged high fees for their services. A man might have to give two horses for a difficult spell.

A Medicine Man was always called in when someone was sick. Although many of his remedies had no medical foundation, patients often felt better, as they believed the magic would work. Singing, chanting and rattles were used to get rid of sickness and bad spirits. The Navajo had a particularly impressive ceremony called sand painting. The Medicine Man spread a layer of sand on the floor of the sick man's home and painted patterns on it with coloured powders. The patient was placed in the middle of the finished picture and everyone chanted spells to drive out the sickness. George Catlin, who watched some magical cures performed by a shaman, was rather cynical about their effectiveness. He said that if the patient recovered, the Medicine Man took the credit, but if he died, it was said to be the will of the Great Spirit.

Medicine Men were also skilled in the use of herbs and drugs. White trappers and settlers often said that their lives had been saved by Indian remedies. A distinguished nineteenth-century explorer, Prince Maximilian, was cured of scurvy when he was given raw garlic bulbs to eat. Mandrake was one of the herbal cures and used as a purge. Sick Cheyenne children were dosed with a drink made from wild mint. Cree Medicine Men prescribed well-chewed fir-cones for a sore throat. Bruises and cut knees were soothed with an infusion of yarrow by the Ute, and all tribes used a useful ointment made from bear's grease. Quinine and coco were more powerful remedies, and are the basis of some modern drugs.

15

11 A Medicine Man inside the Medicine Lodge, a Plains Indian of the south. In front of him are several sacred pipes.

"Forming Medicine"

Although a Medicine Man was magician for the whole tribe, every boy had to "form" his own medicine. In other words, he had to make contact with the gods himself. Boys were ready for this important stage of their lives at fourteen or fifteen years old. Each boy had to go out into the wild alone, where he fasted for some five days, calling on the Great Spirit to visit him:

> I give my soul to thee, Great Manitou!
> Let mine eyes see a vision of the future
> That I may know myself and my destiny!

Most boys had never before been alone for so long, and the isolation and lack of food made them hypersensitive. If everything went well, they would begin to have visions and see which animal was to be their future guardian spirit. If no vision appeared, the boy would have failed. He would not be able to join a warrior brotherhood, but would be destined to become a servant of his tribe.

Once a boy had discovered which animal was to be his protector, the next stage in forming his medicine was to make a medicine bag. This would become his most precious possession and he would keep it with him always. The bag was made from the skin of his guardian animal. The contents might seem strange to us, but each item had magical significance for its owner. The charms might have been inspired by visions or be relics from battles. Sometimes they were family charms. A child's own umbilical cord was always dried and kept as a powerful talisman. A warrior carried his medicine

bag into battle and was disgraced if it was captured. He could only be reinstated as a warrior by recapturing it, or by seizing someone else's bag. The magical power of a medicine bundle was much stronger than that of a lucky charm. It was more like a personal guardian angel. As George Catlin wrote, the bundle was a man's "strength in battle", and at death it was buried with him, "to conduct him safe to the beautiful hunting grounds, which he contemplates in the world to come".

Friendly and protective animals
Indians thought of animals as their brothers. If they killed an animal while hunting, they explained to it that the killing had been for food and not sport. Actual words were not always necessary, because Indians believed an animal could understand what they were thinking. An Indian told Arthur Parker in the 1920s:

The animals are not wild; it's men who are

12   Whirling log sand painting, by a Navajo Indian. Sand paintings were used in curing the sick.

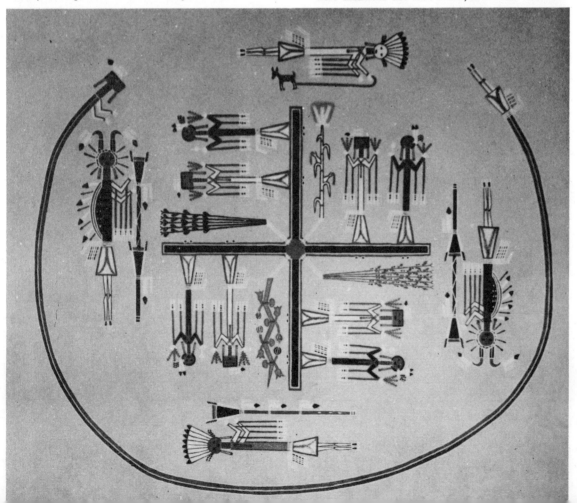

wild and frighten them. Animals know what men think and know when the hunter wants to kill them and so they run.

According to Indian mythology, animals and men could change shapes with each other at will. Many people had been animals in a previous existence. As a Winnebago Medicine Man once said:

I came from above and I am holy. This is my second life on earth .... At one time I became transformed into a fish. At another time I became a buffalo. From my buffalo existence I was permitted to go to my higher spirit-home, from which I had originally come.

13 Medicine Men were skilled in the use of herbs. This Chippewa Medicine Man was drawn preparing herbs to treat a patient.

Before white settlers populated North America, Indians led quiet lives in isolated communities. The landscape was wild and strange. The nights were long and dark. Animals were warm and living, like men, and natural allies in the wilderness. All children had an animal guardian spirit. This protector was called a totem. Apart from a personal totem, children also had family and tribal totems, all of which might be different animals. This gave each child a spiritual family of totems, rather like his own family and tribe. Symbols of his magical protectors were included in his medicine bundle, and they would also be represented in any paintings or carvings that he did. Some animals were thought to have special magical powers. A badger could foretell the future. A cricket might be used to show where the buffalo herds could be found. Eagles and hawks,

soaring above the earth, could give advice in time of war, like reconnaissance aircraft today.

The tribes of the North West Coast carved their animal protectors on totem poles. The totem poles, which were often built into the houses, were in a very real sense family trees. The carved animals represented the guardian spirits of a man's ancestors — the more animals that appeared, the more his family was worthy of respect. Totem poles were very impressive and really looked like guardian spirits. The animals seemed to have a ferocious magical strength, particularly in the Haida territory, where they were carved from especially large trees.

Masks and magic

Perhaps the most impressive magical ceremonies that a child would see were the tribal dances. Sometimes people danced to bring the sun or rain to the crops, or to gain success in hunting. Other dances were performed before going into battle. The Ghost Dance was an old ceremony, revived in the nineteenth century during war with white settlers. In it the dancers conjured

14 This model of a wooden house of the Haida tribe of the North West Coast shows the totem pole built into the house. The carvings on the totem pole represented the family's guardian spirits.

15 The Ghost Dance.

16 The Hopi tribe of the Pueblo Indians perform the Kachina dance, c.1900.

up their ancestors and the spirits of dead buffalo to help them to clear the enemy from their land. Performers wore magical ghost shirts to protect them from bullets. A child watching a ceremonial dance would forget that the masked and strangely dressed dancers were members of his family and friends. They would be transformed into the animals they represented.

The Iroquois had particularly hideous masks to protect themselves from ghosts who lived in the forests. These creatures had no bodies, only ghastly rolling heads. The masks were known as "False Faces" and, when not in use, were kept wrapped up in white cloths, face downwards on the ground, and had to be fed regularly. Other strange masks made by the Iroquois were constructed out of corn husks, and used in agricultural ceremonies. All kinds of gods and spirits were represented by masks throughout America. Apart from the Iroquois masks, some of the strangest were made by Indians on the North West Coast. Many of these were of strange sea monsters, like Yagis, who the Kwakiutl believed liked to capsize canoes and eat the occupants.

At a feast or celebration a Medicine Man would perform tricks. These were like our stage magic and included ventriloquism and fire-swallowing. Some shamans would develop their powers of telepathy by fasting or taking drugs, and would try to see into the future. Many of the strange ceremonies would seem remote to a child, who would feel much closer to his animal guardian. Pueblo children also understood "kachina" spirits, which the Indians of the South West believed in. They looked after crops, rain and sunlight, and were represented by kachina dolls, which were given to small Pueblo children to keep them safe.

▲
17 Straw mask of the Iroquois Indians.

18 Painted wooden mask with moveable eyes ▶
and lower jaw, of the Tsimhain tribe of the North West Coast.

21

3 Everyday Life

Nineteenth-century North American Indians did not live in towns like their contemporaries in Europe. Except in the South West, where some of the buildings were made of stone, houses were not built to last. Although an Indian settlement might only be temporary, great care was taken to choose a good site. A camp must be near water and a ready food supply. It was also important to find a sheltered situation which could be defended if enemies attacked. Between one hundred and three hundred people lived in an average Indian village.

19   A Pueblo village in New Mexico. The dome shapes in the foreground are ovens.

In Catlin's day Indians were still living quiet, isolated lives. There were no roads linking the villages. People travelled on horseback, by canoe or on foot. Many of the tribesmen of the Great Plains, who were hunters, had no permanent homes but followed the buffalo herds. Most Indians had few personal possessions, little furniture and lived communal lives. They got up at sunrise. Not much could be done after dark and winter nights were long and cold. The same cycle of events — the spring sowing, the harvest, the movement of the buffalo herds — marked the passing of each year. Past time was calculated from significant events, like "The Winter the Stars Fell", which referred to a shower of meteorites in 1833.

Indian homes

Although the Pueblos of North Arizona and New Mexico lived in settlements similar in size and permanence to the villages of the Old World, their houses looked quite different. The buildings were made of sandstone and cemented together with mud called adobe. Frank Hamilton Cushing, who lived in a Zuni village during 1897, described the

> numberless long, box-like shapes, adobe ranches, connected with one another in extended rows and squares, with others, less and less numerous, piled upon them lengthwise and crosswise, in two, three, even six stories, each receding from the one below it like the steps of a broken stair-flight.

The front door was generally on the first

20 Plains Indians' tepees, with a cooking fire outside.

floor so as to keep out thieves. People got in by climbing a long ladder, which they pulled up after them. The lower floors, which were dark and unheated, were used for storage. Upstairs the rooms were quite snug. Each had a small fire under a smoke hole, and floors were covered with mats and rugs.

Most people know what the tepee homes of the Plains Indians looked like. They were tents rather than houses, could be erected quickly and transported easily by means of a travois. They were not necessarily the owner's only home as many hunters returned to village huts in the winter. The framework of a tepee was a number of poles tied together at the top to make a cone shape, leaving a hole for smoke from the fire to

21 The wigwams or "wickieups" of this Iroquoian settlement were made of elm bark.

escape. A cover of buffalo hide was fastened to the frame, leaving a door flap, and the hide was pegged to the ground. Hunters of the Plains, like the Sioux and Blackfoot, painted pictures in bright colours on the outside of their tepees. There was room for little more than the beds inside. A central fire provided heat, and the tent's ventilation flaps could be pulled up to force smoke out through the smoke hole, instead of into everyone's eyes. A tent flap acted as the front door and outsiders had to ask permission before going in. The word "wigwam", often used instead of "tepee", only applies, in fact, to a different kind of building with a rounded roof, covered with woven mats or birch bark. Wigwams were common among the Apaches in the South West and were also known as "wickieups".

Farming tribes like the Mandan lived in earth lodges. These houses had a sturdy wooden framework on which turfs of grass and earth were laid. The buildings were circular and would hold about thirty people. The roofs were strong enough to walk on, and in fine weather families gathered up there to talk and to enjoy a grandstand view of village life. Inside, the floor was hollowed out round a central fireplace. This left ready-made earth benches at floor level, for people to sit on to eat and talk round the fire. Separate families had their own living quarters in the lodge, screened with skins and rugs. The main piece of furniture was a low wooden bed, piled high with rugs and furs. Dry grass was sometimes used as a mattress or to fill

22 A Mandan village, showing people sitting on ➤ the roofs of their earth lodges. Drawn by George Catlin.

24

the pillows. A bedhead was made from woven willow twigs. Beside each bed was a post where personal possessions could be hung, such as a bow, gun, medicine bag or tobacco pouch. Special treasures were often hidden in a hole dug beneath the bed. Clothing was stuffed away behind the bed and in odd corners. Earth lodges were suited to the climate of the northern plains and prairies as they could be kept cool in summer and warm in winter. The Navajo of the South West still live in a variety of earth lodge known as a "hogan".

Forest dwellers, like the Iroquois, naturally built wooden houses, as there was plenty of raw material available. Most villages were surrounded by a wooden stockade to keep out intruders. Some of the buildings had rounded roofs and others were known as "longhouses" and had pitched roofs. Longhouses could be as much as

23   A drawing of a longhouse, from Arthur C. Parker's *The Indian How Book.*

35 metres in length. Inside, each family had its own fire and smoke hole. In winter everyone huddled round the fire to sleep, but in summer they slept on wooden

benches along each side of the house to avoid fleas. On the North West Pacific Coast the Haida and Tlingit built more elaborate wooden houses, decorated with carving and usually with a totem pole attached.

Tribal customs and government

At the end of the eighteenth century there were about six hundred different Indian tribes, speaking three hundred different languages, in North America. Children growing up in one Indian village would know little about children of other tribes living a short distance away. If they did meet, they might only be able to communicate in sign language. A child's loyalty would be first to his own family and clan of relations. After that would come his loyalty to his village. Members of the same tribe would be scattered over a wide area in many different villages. Sometimes the various groups would act together, like the six tribes who banded together to form the Iroquois Confederacy in the seventeenth century. However, joint decisions were rare, although members of the same tribe would feel kinship with one another.

Within a village the chief did not necessarily have absolute power. A council of elders decided policy and administered justice. Punishments for crime varied in different parts of the country. George Catlin found the Indians he met during his travels in the 1830s extremely honest. He wrote:

I have travelled several years already among these people and I have not had my scalp taken, nor a blow struck me; nor had occasion to raise my hand against an Indian; nor has my property been stolen . . . and that in a country where no man is punishable by law for the crime of stealing.

Sometimes, even crimes as serious as murder were left to the victim's relations to avenge.

On the other hand, the Huron tribes of the Great Lakes area worked out an elaborate system of fines. If a warrior was killed, thirty presents had to be paid to his relations. The blood price for a woman was forty presents, as she was less able to defend herself. The highest fine was for the murder of a stranger, as this might lead to war or stop trading. A mid-nineteenth-century traveller called Edwin Denig described an amusing method used by the Crow to deal with petty offences. He said:

Smaller pilfering and discord are decided by heartily abusing each other . . . . Most of these expressions consist of comparing the visage and person thus abused to the most disgusting objects in nature . . .

Family life

The family was the centre of a child's life. As there were no schools, all education and training for adult life was given at home. Children had happy lives when they were very young, as the Indians loved and indulged them. A ducking in the river was the worst punishment given to a child. Children were never spanked. Grandparents were respected for their wisdom and generally named a new baby.

The centre of family life was the fire, where food was cooked and people gathered round to talk and keep warm. The fire was so important for well-being that there were many legends connected with it. Some tribes had a Keeper of the Flame to see that the fire was always kept alight. It was considered rude to pass between the master of the house and the fire. A good way to kindle a fire was to twirl a stick into a notch on another stick until the friction produced a spark which could be used to set alight some dried grass or bark. Another method was to strike two flints together. The fire was kept low for safety and for cooking. The Indians say: "Little fire, get close, cook easy; big fire, keep away, burn

everything, cook nothing — no good."

Indians had little furniture apart from a bed, which might be only a pile of skins on the ground. Children usually slept at the foot of their parents' bed. The bedhead was used as a backrest during the day. Houses were on one level, except in the Pueblo villages, and flooring was simply beaten earth, swept and polished until it shone. Woven mats and rugs provided extra warmth and comfort. In fine weather most jobs, like weaving and pottery, were done outside. During the long winter nights, people gathered round the fire to tell stories and play games.

Most Indians took frequent baths. Forest Indians thought that water made a child grow strong, and Iroquois babies were bathed daily. The most convenient way to take a bath was to swim in a lake or river.

24　Inside a Mandan earth lodge, by George Catlin. Separate sleeping cabins are shown in the background.

Another method was to strip and then jump about in the rain. Sometimes boys took a mud bath. They covered themselves with wet mud which they let dry in the sun. Then they peeled off the baked layer and jumped into the river. Warriors and athletes were given special oil baths by the Medicine Man. Northern tribes rubbed themselves in snow. Hunters bathed in water containing sweet ferns, to remove any bodily smell that an animal might detect. Young warriors took sweat baths for ritual purposes in special "sweat houses". Steam was produced by heating stones on a roaring fire outside a tent or hut. The stones were then lifted into the sweat house with special sticks, and water was thrown onto them. Gradually the hut filled with hissing steam, and the bather stayed there for as long as he could, before rushing out and plunging into the river. If Indians were living in an area where there was little water, they had to manage without a bath. Then the only way to get clean was to rub themselves with sand or ashes to remove the dirt.

Death

Indians lived for the present moment, and had a practical view of death and illness. They thought that life after death would be very similar to their present existence. George Catlin described the Chocktaw belief that a spirit must travel after death towards the west, where he would find:

25 An Indian burial ground on the Mississippi. The corpses were placed on trees or platforms, out of the way of wolves.

the good hunting grounds, where there is one continual day — where the trees are always green . . . where there is no pain or trouble, and people never grow old, but for ever live young and enjoy the youthful pleasures.

Dead relatives were mourned and ancestors respected. If a baby died, a mother would fill the cradle with black quills and mourn the child for a year. However, there was also a harshly practical side to the nomadic Indians. Old people who might become a burden to a tribe on the move were abandoned, in a simple shelter with some food, to die alone. George Catlin tells of an old chief saying goodbye to his friends in this way: "My children, our nation is poor, and it is necessary that you should all go to the country where you can get meat . . . . Keep your hearts stout, and think not of me."

4 Eating and Drinking

Captain John Smith was full of enthusiasm about the variety of food available for white settlers when he landed in Virginia in 1607. He mentioned the plentiful game — deer, partridge, "wild turkies as big as our tame", and the swans, cranes, herons, geese and ducks. In the rivers and in the sea there were sturgeon, mullet, salmon, trout, plaice, herring, lobster and shellfish of all kinds. "Virginia doth afford many excellent vegetables and living creatures," he wrote. He also listed fruits, nuts and berries.

In some parts were found some chestnuts, whose wild fruit equal the best in France . . . . Plums there are of three sorts. The red and white are like our hedge plums, but the other, which they call 'putchamins', grow as high as a palmetto . . . . If it be not ripe, it will draw a man's mouth awry, with much torment; but when it is ripe, it is as delicious as an apricot.

When the Pilgrim Fathers landed in New England in 1620, they were in poor physical condition and found it hard to live off the land. They owed their survival to the help they received from some Indians, who taught them how to fish, to stalk game and, most important of all, to plant corn. Gradually the settlers learnt how to use the new fruits and vegetables which grew wild, and how to cook the Indian way, over a camp fire or in a hole in the ground. Many foodstuffs commonly used today were first grown in America and eaten by the Indians.

The most important of these was maize, which the Indians called "bread of life" or "grain of the gods". Potatoes were also native to the American continent. Sweet potatoes were being cultivated in Virginia when the first settlers arrived, but ordinary potatoes were introduced into Europe from South America, by the Spanish explorers. Tomatoes, squashes and all kinds of beans were also American in origin. Indian recipes which have been adapted for use today include "hominy grits", a kind of porridge made from fine-ground corn and eaten for breakfast by modern Americans. "Hasty Pudding" and "Indian Pudding" are still popular dishes, both made from corn meal. Corn on the cob, baked beans and "succotash" (a mixture of fish, corn and beans) were first eaten by Indians. They were also the first to use maple syrup as a sweetener.

When George Catlin travelled through the Upper Missouri area in the 1830s, he noticed a profusion of wild fruits everywhere. He wrote:

here and there, in every direction, there were little copses and clusters of plum trees and gooseberries and wild currants, loaded down with their fruit.

The Indians he met were skilled at living off the land. They hunted for their meat, gathered their vegetables and fruits in the forests and on the plains, and fished in the rivers and lakes. Some tribes also cultivated corn, squashes and beans in a small way.

From an early age, children helped in the search for food. Small boys were taught to trap and hunt, as these skills were essential for survival. Indians enjoyed eating meat, although a fresh supply was not always available. They stored as much as they could, to use in the winter. Elk, deer, antelope and beaver flesh were eaten, but the main delicacy was buffalo meat. A beaver's tail was highly thought of for special occasions. Pigeons and other birds were shot for food, and rabbits and various small animals like hedgehogs, lizards and even insects might also be found in the cooking pot. Dog meat was eaten as a treat, and Catlin noticed how it "sent forth a very savoury and pleasant smell" when stewed.

Although Indians liked to gorge themselves with food after a successful hunting expedition, they made sure that some meat was preserved for the winter. Buffalo flesh was cured, but not by using salt or smoke as the practice is today. The meat was cut into strips and hung out in the sun on special stands to dry, out of the way of dogs. "Pemmican" was made by pounding up dried buffalo meat into a fine powder and mixing it with ground cherry stones, melted fat and marrow. Stored in a bag called a "parfleche", it could be kept for years and was nourishing and tasty. Fish was treated in the same way. The cranberry, called "sassamanesh" by Indians, was often used in pemmican and this is the origin of the use of cranberry sauce with turkey and meats today.

Marrow fat extracted from broken buffalo bones was an Indian delicacy particularly enjoyed by white men when they were invited to Indian feasts. George Catlin relates how

at feasts, chunks of this marrow-fat are

27 Indians fishing from a dug-out canoe in Virginia. Drawn by John White, 1585-1590.

cut off and placed in a tray or bowl, with the pemmican, and eaten together, which we civilised folks in these regions consider a very good substitute for . . . 'bread and butter'.

As the marrow fat was bright yellow in colour, it did look rather like butter.

Meat was generally cooked over an open fire, by boiling or frying. On feast days

28 Buffalo meat drying on a special rack.

large cuts of meat were roasted on spits. The few cooking pots that women owned were made of clay, but they were strong enough to stand up to open flames. Indians enjoyed their food and praised a good cook. One cooking method which increased the flavour of a dish was to seal the meat in a thick layer of clay and place it in the embers of the fire. Skin and feathers were kept on during cooking as they would come away with the clay when it was broken. There was also the hole in the ground method of cooking. Catlin describes how the Assinniboins lined a hole with raw hide and filled it with water. A cooking bowl containing raw meat was placed in the water which was heated by taking hot stones from a nearby fire and dropping them in. This slowly braised the meat. Clams were sometimes cooked in a hole in the rocks on the seashore. A fire was lit in the hole and allowed to burn out. Food was placed into the warm, oven-like place, in a loosely woven container. Layers of wet seaweed were placed over it, and a heavy cloth put on top, so that the clams would gradually cook in the steam.

From an early age, small girls helped their mothers with the cooking. They were also sent out to gather nuts, berries and roots. In some parts of America such as California, where little meat was available, these would be the only food to eat for most of the year. In the woodlands wild blueberries, huckleberries, blackberries, cherries and strawberries could be found. All kinds of nuts were gathered, and flour was made from acorns and chestnuts. The flour was made into bread or a watery porridge. Walnuts were crushed to extract the oil. Seeds, roots and the tender shoots of plants were also eaten. Women had special digging tools to extract root vegetables like the wild potato or prairie turnip. Mushrooms and other edible fungi were gathered, and even the bark of trees could be used for food, if cut up and boiled to make soup. Wild rice could be found in the Great Lakes area. Indians gathered it from their canoes, shaking the grains into the bottom of the boat.

Women were responsible in most tribes for any crops that were grown. Maize, known today as "Indian corn", was the most popular crop. The tribal Medicine Man would announce the day on which the green corn was ready to be gathered. The corn was boiled in kettles amid feasting and singing, and the first kettleful was offered to the Great Spirit. The rest of the corn was left to ripen and was later ground into flour for bread.

At mealtimes Indians sat cross-legged on the ground round the fire, or lay on buffalo robes. Women looked after the men and ate later. Everyone had his own bowl, spoon and knife. Forks were not used. Food was ladled straight from the cooking pot into individual bowls. The dogs prowled about looking for scraps. It was polite to show enjoyment and a rule to offer hospitality to strangers. George Catlin was entertained many times by Indian tribes. On one occasion, when eating with the Mandan, he had a three-course meal, starting with pemmican and marrow fat, with roasted buffalo ribs as the main course and a pudding made from prairie turnips flavoured with berries.

Indian eating habits were not greatly

29 A Nez Perce woman making pemmican at a temporary encampment of a small hunting party on the Yellowstone River.

30 A basket made of reed woven into willow twigs and used for gathering berries and nuts for food.

influenced by white settlers in the nineteenth century. Cattle were first introduced into the continent by the Spanish in South America, and later spread to Texas and South California, where they were hunted like other animals. Indians began gradually to use new cooking utensils, such as frying pans, which they obtained through trade. Their drinking habits were more adversely affected. In the past they had drunk only water and herbal teas for medicinal purposes — Indians have always disliked drinking milk. Then the fur traders introduced them to whiskey and rum and, as the Indians were not used to alcohol, much drunkenness and misery was caused.

31 Indian women gathering wild rice from their canoe.

5 The Life of an Indian Girl

Indian girls were expected to work hard all through their lives, but in some ways their position in society was better than that of European women in the nineteenth century. Although boys and girls had different tasks, there was a fair division of labour. Women were treated with courtesy, and usually owned the family's living quarters and household possessions. Ancestors were generally traced through the female line. Iroquois women, who were particularly privileged, had the right to nominate chieftains and could vote in council. On the other hand, Crow and Blackfoot women, according to George Catlin, were

> the slaves of their husbands, being obliged to perform all the domestic duties and drudgeries of the tribe, and not allowed to join in their religious rites or ceremonies, nor in the dance or other amusements.

They were also expected to cover their faces when strangers were about.

Education
All children played together during their early years. Teaching began when they reached the age of five, but it was not formal schooling as we know it. Teaching was by example, and given by parents and relatives. Boys went out with the male members of the family and learnt to ride and shoot. Girls were taken in hand by their mothers and shown how to cook and sew. They were given dolls and small models of household

32 Young girls were given toys, like this Navajo model of a woman weaving, to help them understand their future work.

articles. They were taught how to make small cooking pots with lumps of clay. Gradually, through play, they became accustomed to doing the tasks that they would have to perform in the future. A girl's first responsible jobs were to gather firewood and collect water. Usually a group of girls went off together and it became quite a social occasion.

A girl became a grown-up member of the tribe after her first menstruation. Among the Cheyenne the occasion was marked with a special ceremony. The girl bathed, loosened her hair, and her body was painted red. Then she sat beside a herb-scented fire and let the smoke blow over her. After this, she went to a special lodge where she was instructed in womanly conduct by her grandmother. Her coming of age was announced to the tribe, and her family started to make marriage plans.

33 Indian dolls in buckskin costume, of the Klikitat Indians of the North West Coast.

Marriage

As women did most of the work around camp, a daughter was a valuable possession. Fathers showed their love by offering a good dowry to a prospective bridegroom. In return, a suitor offered goods to the father to compensate for the loss of his daughter's labour. George Catlin describes how one father was offered two horses and a gun, with powder and shot for a year. Another suitor gave six pounds (3 Kg) of beads, plus two gallons (9 litres) of whiskey in return for his bride. Although marriages were arranged by parents, a girl could usually make her feelings known before a formal proposal was made. An Iroquois girl usually confided in her mother the name of the man she wanted to marry. The two mothers would then get together to discuss marriage prospects. If the boy and girl were both happy with the proposal, the girl would hang up a basket of "bride's biscuits" at the door, and the man would eat one as a marriage pledge. There was plenty of opportunity for romance and flirtation before and during courtship. Sioux young men played flutes to cast a spell over the girl they desired. On summer nights love songs could be heard: "My love, come out into the prairie, so that I may come near you and meet you." Plains Indians had a courtship custom involving a blanket, which nearly got an artist called William Carey into trouble in 1861. He had left the steamer on which he was travelling to sketch an Indian squaw on the river bank. He was told that he had taken part in a marriage ceremony because he had placed a blanket on her shoulders to make his painting more colourful. Hurriedly he got back on board the steamer, reasoning "that if getting married was as easy as all that, divorce could be just as simple".

There was no uniform marriage ceremony among American Indians, and all tribes had slightly different customs. Sometimes there was only a formal exchange of

34 Eeh-nis-kin, the favoured wife of the Blackfoot chief, according to George Catlin.

gifts, but usually a wedding was an excuse for feasting and merrymaking, as it is in all countries. The bride's hair was plaited, her face painted, and she was dressed in her best clothes and jewellery by female relatives. Occasionally an ancient form of marriage called "marriage by capture" was performed, where the bridegroom and his friends pretended to carry the girl off by force. In some parts of the country, where there were more women than men, husbands were allowed more than one wife. Chiefs and Medicine Men might have as many as fourteen wives, as a sign of wealth and prestige. Wives sometimes welcomed the help of another woman with the family tasks. But there must sometimes have been rivalry if one wife was specially favoured, like Eeh-nis-kin, who was painted by George Catlin, and was one of the wives of a Blackfoot chief. Catlin said that the girl was "the apple of his eye" and exempt "from the drudgeries of the camp".

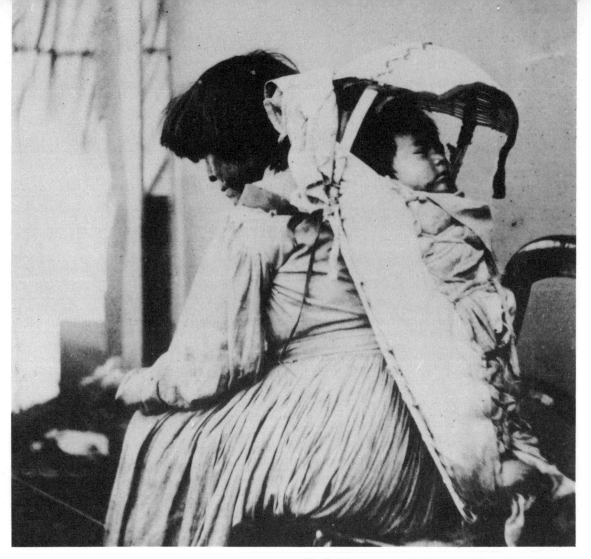

35 Babies were carried in a cradleboard on their mother's back.

Babies

Indian women of Catlin's time generally had two or three children. Many babies died at birth. During labour the mother retired to a special hut. She prayed to the birth goddess, saying: "You came into this life with ease. Do what you can for me now, that my child may be born the same way." Children were sometimes breast-fed until they were four years old. Indian mothers liked to keep their babies with them all the time. The Indian equivalent of the modern baby sling was the cradleboard. Although the stiff cradle looks uncomfortable, babies seemed to enjoy it and could watch from it all that was going on. The board was convenient, as it could be strapped to the mother's back when she was working or left propped up beside a tree or other support. Even at home the baby stayed in the cradle, although the straps were untied, and the child could play with the bits of tinsel and shining coins that were attached to the headpiece. Cheyenne mothers did not like to hear their children crying, particularly as the noise might give away the tribe's position

to an enemy. A crying child was taken outside and brought back only when the crying had stopped. Children were not always named straight away after birth. The Medicine Man's advice was often sought, as names were thought to have magical significance.

Work

Women knew that they would be constantly at work and would have little time for leisure. They were responsible not only for feeding the family, but also for growing any vegetables they might need and for cutting up the meat into joints after a hunt. They would also dry the meat for storage.

36 A woman of the Sioux tribe of Dakota working on a buffalo skin.

Before every meal, wood for the fire and water had to be collected. Berries and nuts must be gathered in the forest. Women also made all the family's clothes. This was not merely a case of dressmaking or weaving. It also meant skinning the animals after a hunt and dressing the hides. These were exhausting and messy jobs. First the flesh was removed from the hide with a fleshing tool. Then the skins were soaked and the hair removed. Later, hides were stretched on frames to dry in the open air or were smoked by a fire. Buckskin, which was used

and spent a good deal of time embroidering their garments with beads or porcupine quills. They wore long or short skirts, or buckskin robes which might be fringed and have painted decoration. A man whose wife was a good embroideress was greatly envied, and Cheyenne women had a special society for experts in the art. In Navajo country and the South West woven garments were sometimes worn.

Dress varied very much according to the climate. Both sexes wore moccasins, which are soft shoes made from one piece of raw hide and stitched with sinew. Often they were embroidered with beads. Fur robes and leggings were usually worn in winter. Women wore their hair in two plaits, but unmarried women sometimes put it up in the "squash blossom" style. They were proud of their long, black hair which their husbands helped to dress. Most Indians wore plenty of jewellery and Navajo silverwork was particularly beautiful. Face paint took the place of cosmetics and elaborate designs were created with paints made from vegetable or mineral dyes. As they lived an active life, women were rarely fat. They bathed regularly and swam naked in the forest streams. Many of the early explorers wrote about the beauty of Indian girls, and some married them. An explorer, Francis Parkman described a Sioux girl he met in 1846 whose clothes would seem attractive today. The girl had a "light, clear complexion, enlivened by a spot of vermilion on each cheek . . . . Her dress was a tunic of deerskin made beautifully white by means of a species of clay found on the prairie, ornamented with beads, arranged in figures more gay than tasteful, and with long fringes at all the seams."

for clothes, was worked until it was extremely soft and pliable. It was also waterproof.

As women were responsible for looking after the home, moving camp was a particularly busy time for them. George Catlin described how the women all walked together with their loads, while the men rode in a lordly way beside them and "never lend a hand".

Clothes
Indian girls liked to wear beautiful clothes,

6 Young Warriors

An Indian boy's family expected him to become a warrior and hunter when he grew up. Although boys and girls played together until adolescence, boys were taught separately by their fathers and male relations, and had small bows and arrows as their toys. Francis Parkman described a Sioux village that he visited in 1846, where the children were "whooping about the camp, shooting birds with little bows and arrows, or making miniature lodges with sticks". There were many practical things to learn: for example, making a fire, following a trail, signalling, plaiting a rope, carving wood and bone, riding a horse and managing a canoe. Later on, when he was far away from his friends and family, a boy would have to know how to look after himself. It was particularly important to ride a horse well. Many Indians rode bareback, but some preferred to use elaborately decorated saddles. A horse was an Indian's most valuable possession and was celebrated in this Sioux warrior's song:

> My horse be swift in flight
> Even like a bird
> My horse be swift in flight
> Bear me now in safety
> Far from the enemy's arrows.
> And you shall be rewarded
> With streamers and ribbons red.

Practical training

As there were no roads, boys had to learn how to follow a trail. They were taught to notice the small signs made with twigs or

38 A six-year old Blackfoot boy, drawn by George Catlin. His robe was made of racoon skin.

stones which an ordinary person might not spot. They must also be able to mark a new trail and to obliterate their tracks if an enemy was following. They had to develop an acute sense of hearing and smell, so that they could identify men or animals which

41

to "freeze" to escape detection. A good trick to put off a pursuer was to lay a false trail or to "back-track" — a way of making your tracks look as if they were heading in the opposite direction. All forest Indians learnt how to swim, and could hide by swimming under water, sometimes beneath a log of wood.

Skill in signalling was important too. Indians kept in touch with each other by signalling with puffs of smoke from wood fires. To do this, a fire was damped down with grass, and two people held a blanket on and off it to create small smoke clouds which could be seen from far away. Messages could be sent in relays over great distances from one party of Indians to another. At night torches or fire arrows were used instead. Fire arrows were ordinary arrows with the tips wrapped in tow dipped in oil. A bark fuse, glued to the arrow shaft, lit when the arrow was fired. Among the Santee, one arrow meant "the enemy is about", two arrows indicated "danger" and three "great danger". If several arrows were fired, it was a sign that the enemy was too strong and the party was retreating.

There were many hunting skills to be learnt. Boys were taught to make ingenious snares and traps. A good way to trap a large animal like a deer was to dig a deep pit and disguise it with bracken, so that the animal fell in. Sometimes a noose was hung from a tree, to catch a deer as it ran. Large logs were balanced so that they would fall on a creature if the supporting sticks were disturbed. Fishing was another skill which could be learnt young. Boys were not allowed out with a big hunting expedition until they had proved that they could ride and shoot.

Wood was the main material used by Indians for the necessities of life. It was needed for tent poles, dug-out canoes, dishes, log houses, bows and stockades.

might threaten them. They had to be able to recognize which tribe another Indian they met belonged to. Most of the games that small boys played were meant to test their memories and powers of observation and help them to learn the secret language of the trail.

Boys were also taught how to escape if they should be chased by an enemy or wild animal. It was easier to hide in the forest, by climbing a tree or by creeping into a hollow trunk. On the open prairie the long grass could be used as cover. If there was nothing at all to hide in, boys were taught

40 Two Indian traps drawn by Arthur C. Parker ▶ in *The Indian How Book,* 1927. Top: the large logs were balanced so that they would fall on the animal which disturbed the sticks. Bottom: the noose would catch a deer as it ran.

It was also wanted for cooking and heating. Boys learnt how to chop down trees, using a stone axe. First, a fire had to be built round the base of the tree. Then the trunk was plastered with clay to stop the fire from going too high. When the flames had burnt out, it was easy to chip away the charred wood at the bottom of the tree and bring it down. During the nineteenth century primitive Indian tools were gradually being replaced with iron implements obtained through trading with settlers, which made tasks like tree-felling easier.

Training for war

A boy's life became harder when he reached ten or eleven years of age, as it was time to learn to become a warrior as well as a hunter. Indians admired courage and endurance in a man, and a boy had to prove that he was worthy of joining the other braves. Some tribes played special toughening-up games. The Sioux invented a kicking game which was very simple. Two teams lined up and everyone tried to kick someone on the other side. There were no holds barred, including kicking your opponent in the face, and the game finished when everyone was exhausted. A Sioux called Iron Shell described the game to Arthur Parker in the 1920s, saying: "Some boys got badly hurt, but afterwards we would talk and laugh about it. Very seldom did any fellows get angry." Apache Indians, who were particularly fond of fighting, had special endurance tests. Young men had to run in hot weather with a mouthful of water which they were not allowed to drink. They also had mock battles with real arrows.

Indians liked to belong to clubs which were similar to secret societies. There was a club or lodge for each age group and for every totem. Clubs for young boys were rather like the Boy Scouts. Members divided up into companies and competed with each other. A boy could join a warrior society only after he had proved himself in battle. Once admitted to his chosen society, he would be bound in brotherhood to other members for the rest of his life.

A boy went on his first raiding party with his father or other male relation. His job was to look after the raiders' horses and to collect wood for the camp fire. It would be an exciting time for him. Before the raid

43

41 Two young Kickapoo Indians, training for war, 1890s.

special war paint was put on and war dances were performed. The party left during the night, carrying their rations. Unless they had bought guns from white settlers, their only weapons were bows and arrows and knives, which they had made themselves. Even tomahawks and scalping knives made of steel were not traditional weapons, but were obtained by trading. Warriors carried a shield for protection, which was made from layers of raw hide stretched over a wooden frame. The shield was often padded with hair or feathers, and painted with magical signs. A raiding party was well disciplined. Creek Indians marched in

44

single file, each man stepping in the footprints of the man in front of him. Raiders had to take the enemy by surprise and usually attacked at night. The aim was to inflict as much damage as possible in the shortest possible time. Afterwards the raiding party split up to make pursuit more difficult. The same principles applied when the attackers were on horseback.

War for the Indians was not fought for quite the same reasons as in the Old World, although the results might be equally fatal. Apart from the usual purposes of gain or defence, some tribes made war because they actually enjoyed it. A raid was a way of showing courage, and killing was avoided if possible. Bravery was demonstrated by "making a coup", which meant touching an enemy with the hand or with a special coup stick. Prisoners were often taken. The women and children were shared out among the tribe, but an unfortunate result of Indian admiration for courage and endurance was the way in which some of the male prisoners were tortured. A captive was respected if he showed no signs of pain and fear, and his bravery gave his captor more glory. One of the nastiest trophies brought back by warriors, to add to their prestige, was an enemy's scalp. This was the skin and hair from the crown of the head, where Indians thought a man's soul existed. Scalping was not necessarily fatal and some victims survived, often to be sent back to their camp as an insult to their tribe. Scalps were cleaned and dried and then carried on poles at ceremonial occasions. They were also used to ornament robes and harnesses. Horses were the most valuable plunder

42 "Making a coup", a painting by Frederic Remington.

Clothes

Indian boys were great dandies and enjoyed showing off their battle trophies in their costume. Scalps were used for fringing robes, and buckskin garments were painted with pictures of the owner's brave deeds. Hunting trophies were also used. Bear's teeth were made into necklaces, and buffalo horns and eagle feathers adorned headdresses. Wolfskins and bearskins became cloaks. Eagle feather headdresses were especially significant as each feather signified a coup. Costume varied according to tribe, but a basic form of clothing was worn throughout North America. Men wore a breechcloth, over which they placed a shirt or robe of buckskin. Leggings were worn, except in very hot climates, and moccasins on the feet. In the South West the Pueblo dressed almost entirely in woven garments. There was a wide range of cloaks, blankets, sashes and hats of various kinds. Some Indians wore underclothes of fur during the winter and the southern-most tribes stripped down to the breechcloth in summer. Faces and bodies were painted. Each tribe and warrior society had its own symbols, which often took many hours to complete. Indians generally have little facial hair, so there was no shaving problem. Any hairs that did appear were plucked out. Hair was worn long, but it was greased and carefully cut. Some tribes like the Pawnee shaved their heads or cultivated one lock of hair. The Pawnees told George Catlin that before they had purchased scissors, they cut their hair with knives. Before they got knives, "they were in the habit of burning it off with red hot stones, which was a very slow and painful operation".

George Catlin describes in his diary a

stolen on a raid.

Boys were eager to become accepted into a warrior society, as it was the only way to gain status, play some part in government and make a good marriage. One famous warrior society was the Kaitsenko of the Kiowas. They pledged themselves to lead in battle and fight on until victory or death. There were only ten members, and their leader wore a long, black elkskin sash which he pinned to the ground during fighting, so that he would remain there until victory was won. Each secret society had its own rituals and rules, songs and ceremonies. The lodge would be like a club, where men would go for rest and relaxation.

44 The chief of a Blackfoot tribe, Stu-mick-O- ►
Sucks ("The buffalo's back fat").

particularly impressive Assinniboin warrior called Wi-Jun-Jon, whose portrait he painted in St Louis in the 1830s:

his leggings and shirt were of the mountain-goatskin, richly garnished with quills of the porcupine, and fringed with locks of scalps, taken from his enemies' heads. Over these floated his long hair in plaits, that fell nearly to the ground; his head was decked with war-eagle's plumes — his robe was of the skin of the young buffalo bull, richly garnished and emblazoned with the battles of his life.

7 Games and Pastimes

Indians of all ages liked to play competitive games. There was time to spare for these after the hunting season was over, or when the harvest had been gathered, or during winter evenings. Best of all, Indians liked team games, many of which were played on feast days. These were exciting events with people placing bets on their favourite teams. All kinds of games were played, some resembling football, hockey and lacrosse. Indians in eastern America played a game like hockey with a curved stick and a ball made out of deerskin. The Micmac and Malecites played football. In the far north, Eskimo women as well as men played in the football team.

Lacrosse was invented by the American Indians and played from coast to coast. Players used a pole with a net at one end to throw and catch the ball. The Huron and Iroquois used a lacrosse stick much like the one generally popular today, while the Chippewa preferred a much smaller net. Some tribes in the south used two lacrosse

45 Indians playing lacrosse, drawn by Catlin.

48

sticks each, at the same time. George Catlin watched a Chocktaw lacrosse game where each player wore a tail made out of horse-hair or quills, and a mane of horsehair. The game started at 9.00 a.m. and went on for most of the day. Between six hundred and seven hundred people played, and Catlin could only make out a "condensed mass of ball-sticks, and skins, and bloody noses". Some players never saw the ball at all, and the game stopped when one side had scored one hundred.

Girls had their own favourite game called double-ball. Two weights or balls, joined together by a thong, were lifted with a stick with a bent end and thrown into goal. Another team game called "Snow Snake" was a man's game, in which a

46 Horse racing was a popular Indian sport.

"snake" or rod had to be thrown along the snow as far as possible. Games were not always played purely for enjoyment and often also had some magical purpose. A Medicine Man sometimes advised a patient to play a particular game, or to have a game played on his behalf. All kinds of charms were carried by the players of team games, to bring them luck.

Horse racing was popular, particularly among the Comanche, who might stake all their beads, horses and property on a race result. Sioux boys enjoyed a game where the object was to throw members of the opposite side off their horses. No weapons were used and boys stripped naked for the contest. Some tribes like the Chippewa played special war games on horseback, where a player had to make as many coups as possible with his coup stick. George Catlin watched a similar war game played by young Mandan boys between the ages of seven and fifteen. The teams had bows and arrows made from harmless grass. On their heads were small tufts of grass to represent scalps. In the mock fight and scalping, the winner was the boy who took the most scalps, while keeping his own. Archery shoots were designed to test a hunter's skill. An amusing game was to see who could shoot the most arrows in the air at the same time. Other contests, like spear throwing, also helped to train a man for war.

Indoors there were more gambling games,

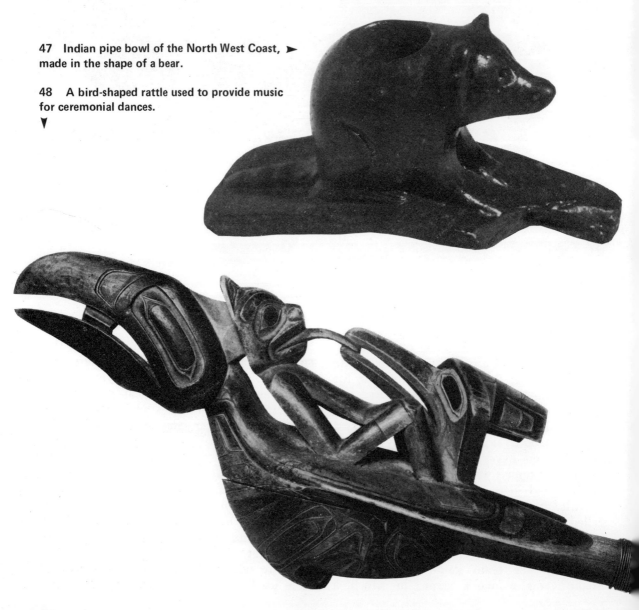

47 Indian pipe bowl of the North West Coast, ► made in the shape of a bear.

48 A bird-shaped rattle used to provide music for ceremonial dances.
▼

49 The Bear Dance of the Plains Indians.

especially after playing-cards had been introduced by white settlers. There were team games like the Cheyenne pastime of passing the button. A token was passed from hand to hand by one team, and at a given moment the other side had to guess who held it. Women had their own amusements, like the awl game, in which players sat in a circle and threw sticks at an awl stone in the centre. Many other popular pastimes included guessing games and cat's cradle, which were played round the camp fire on a winter evening. Best of all, there were the trained story-tellers to amuse everyone, and warriors would boast about their hunting and battle exploits.

A modern way of relaxing, introduced to Europeans by the Indians, was smoking. Even before tobacco was cultivated, Indians smoked weeds, leaves and bark. Pipes were valuable possessions and beautifully made. The pipe bowl was hollowed out from a soft stone, often red in colour, and the stem was made from ash or willow. Elaborate tobacco pouches were made from buckskin. Great significance was attached to smoking and many rituals were associated with it. Alexander Rose, an early fur trapper, noticed how smoking was "the introductory

51

step to all important affairs, and no business can be entered upon with these people before the ceremony of smoking is over." A special pipe of peace called a calumet was passed round when a peace was signed. It was also used in councils, and Catlin noticed how "after the pipe is charged, and is being lit, until the time that the chief has drawn the smoke through it, it is considered an evil omen for anyone to speak."

Indians usually danced and sang for a purpose, rather than just for pleasure. Sometimes it was part of a religious custom, or perhaps it was to celebrate a victory won. Accompaniment was usually on drum, flute or rattle. There were no stringed instruments. George Catlin enjoyed listening to a "mystery whistle", which played in a tone "liquid and sweet beyond description", but he himself was unable to get a sound out of the instrument when he borrowed it from the player. Every member of the tribe must have enjoyed watching the dances and listening to the songs, even if they did not take part. There were dances of all kinds for every sort of occasion — the Buffalo Dance, the Boasting Dance, the Begging Dance, the Eagle Dance, the Sun Dance, the Scalp Dance, and many others. Some were performed by members of a special lodge. Catlin found the dances difficult to understand and thought many were just a "frightful display of starts, and jumps, and yelps". Some of the more picturesque dances were performed by Pueblo Indians in the South West. Their dances had set steps and were carefully rehearsed, unlike those of other tribes, where dancing was much more impromptu. In war dances performers often gave blood-curdling cries.

8 A Buffalo Hunt

Children of the tribes living on the Great Plains would most look forward to a buffalo hunt and the feasting which followed. The lives of the Plains Indians depended on the buffalo herds. Not only did they eat buffalo meat, but every other part of the animal also had a use for them. The hides were sewn into clothes or tents or became covers for canoes. The horns and hoofs were carved into spoons, head ornaments and rattles, or were boiled up to make glue.

Bones were made into sledge runners, arrowheads, hoes, knives, sewing awls and hide-scrapers. Buffalo hair decorated robes and headdresses or made stuffing for mattresses and lacrosse balls. Buffalo fat was used for cooking or was boiled up to make soap. Even the dung was used to burn on fires.

50 Mandan Indians performed the Buffalo Dance before the start of a buffalo hunt.

Because of its value to a tribe, the buffalo was worshipped like a god before a hunt. George Catlin watched the Mandan Indians perform a Buffalo Dance to encourage the herds to come near for the kill. The dancers all wore buffalo heads and imitated the movements of the animal. Sioux Indians danced round an image of a speared buffalo which was painted on the grass. William Carey, an artist in the 1860s, noticed Indians using buffalo skulls resting on plates of water to attract the herds by letting them know that they would not go thirsty if they came.

A buffalo hunt was an exciting time for everyone. Too important to be left to chance, it was organized with military efficiency. First, a council of hunters decided where the hunt should be. Sometimes the whole group moved to a different part of

method was to drive the buffalo towards a snow drift or into a frozen lake, where they would be cornered. Sometimes hunters dressed themselves in wolfskins or buffalo hides and mingled with the herds to lure them into a trap.

Once horses were used, many more buffalo could be killed, but children would not then go with the hunting party, as great riding skill was necessary. The chase could be dangerous, particularly if a hunter fell off into a herd of stampeding animals. Men usually stripped naked for the hunt, apart from a breechcloth, and were armed with a sheath knife, lance or bow. A thong hung from the neck of each horse, and the hunter could catch hold of this if he fell and so slow down his horse in order to remount. Buffalo were trapped by means of a "surround". Two columns of men surrounded the herd and, when the frightened animals stampeded, skilfully turned the leading buffalo round to confuse the other animals. In the resulting chaos, sometimes the buffalo even attacked each other. It usually needed more than one shot to bring down the animals, as they were very powerful. The noise of thundering hoofs and the dust-laden air impressed George Catlin when he took part in a surround with the Minataree Indians. The buffalo herds, enraged by the noise and confusion, turned on the hunters. Catlin saw men escape by throwing their robes over the animals' horns to blind them. In spite of everything, it only took about fifteen minutes to destroy the entire herd. After the battle, Catlin saw the hunters "moving about amongst the dead and dying animals, leading their horses by their halters, and claiming their victims by their private marks upon their arrows, which they were drawing from the wounds in the animals' sides."

After the animals were dead, work began

the country, carrying their tents, bedding and possessions with them. Before Indians had horses, hunting was much more difficult, and they could not travel far and were unable to chase the herd. Instead, they devised ingenious ways of trapping the animals. Sometimes whole tribes, including women and children, rushed towards the buffalo, shouting and waving, and tried to stampede the herd over a cliff. Another

55

52 Hunting the buffalo in the snow. The Indians wear snowshoes.

for the women and children. They carved up the carcasses and removed the hides and cut the meat into suitable joints, while the more perishable parts like the brains and intestines were eaten on the spot, as part of the victory celebrations. Women filled horn cups with the blood, for their children to drink. The hearts were usually left behind on the prairie, as the Indians believed that their magical power would restock the herd. Then the meat and skins were carried back to camp. It was heavy work, but children helped and everyone was excited. Catlin noticed that the party going back to camp with the meat was accompanied by at least "one thousand dogs and puppies . . . whose keen appetites and sagacity had brought them out, to claim their shares of this abundant and sumptuous supply."

9 Cowboys and Indians

By the time George Catlin recorded Indian customs in the 1830s, it was too late for many of the tribes who had already been wiped out by disease and war. Three hundred years of contact with white settlers had changed Indian civilization for good. Both sides feared and despised each other. Catlin, whose sympathies were with the Indians, noted again and again how relationships between the races had been poisoned. For instance, when the explorers Lewis and Clark had first visited the Riccaree

thirty years earlier, the Indians "received and treated them with great kindness and hospitality". Since then fur traders in particular had caused resentment and anger, and the Indians now hated "pale faces". Traders generally tried to swindle Indians by selling them goods at high prices, and giving whiskey and worthless articles in exchange for Indian horses, furs and

53   Lewis and Clark visiting the Riccaree Indians at the beginning of the nineteenth century.

54 Annual summer rendezvous where fur trappers traded with other settlers and with the Indians.

robes. It was the policy of many traders to keep their Indian customers continually in debt and to bribe them with whiskey, which helped to undermine them. Contact between the two races also meant that the Indians were exposed to new diseases, like smallpox, to which they had no resistance.

Naturally there were some beneficial results for Indians from contact with white men. Most important of all was the introduction of horses into the country by the Spanish in 1540. Tribes were no longer so isolated and began to come into contact with other Indian communities as well as with trappers, traders and settlers. The training and sale of horses became an important part of a tribe's economy. Plains Indians were particularly skilled horse-tamers. Catlin, who was himself a competent horseman, found that the wild horses ran off at the sight of him. His Indian friends could lasso an animal, hobble it and then hold a hand over the horse's nose and eyes and breathe into its nostrils, "when it soon becomes docile and conquered; so that he has little else to do then than to remove the hobbles from its feet, and lead or ride it into camp". Unfortunately, Indians seldom got a fair price for their horses from white traders, who, as Catlin said, might exchange them for "a very inferior blanket and butcher's knife". Trade also provided Indians with a new range of tools and weapons. The beautiful woodcarvings of the North West Coast were only possible through the use of European tools. The Old World also brought manufactured beads into the country, which were increasingly used by the Indians to decorate clothes and mocassins, in place of porcupine quills, and which have become so much a part of Indian art. The beads were also used for "wampum", which Indians used for currency, jewellery and ceremonial purposes.

Industrial development in the nineteenth century

George Catlin realized in the 1830s that Indian culture could not stand up to the influence of the sophisticated, energetic and greedy settlers. The next thirty years of the nineteenth century completed the destruction. The main reason for this was the sheer number of immigrants from the Old World. Gradually these settlers moved westwards, occupying land which had before been wild and deserted. The new inhabitants wanted to enclose and farm the land, build

towns, roads and railways. Steamboats carried people and goods along the rivers. Mail coaches, stage coaches and the telegraph helped to link up new communities over the length and breadth of North America. The discovery of gold in California brought an influx of adventurers. Railways helped to create another familiar Hollywood character, the cowboy, whose job was to drive cattle from ranges in the west to railheads like Abilene, for shipment to the towns of the east.

Extinction of the buffalo

Plains Indians were dependent on the buffalo herds for their livelihood, but the animals were gradually being exterminated. This was partly because Indians themselves could hunt more efficiently now that they had horses and guns. But it was also because

55 "The Indian Method of Breaking a Pony", painted by Frederic Remington.

white settlers loved hunting as a sport. In the 1830s Catlin still saw the prairie "actually speckled in distance, and in every direction, with herds of grazing buffalo". He deplored senseless slaughter of the animals by bored soldiers, who killed "these poor creatures in a most cruel and wanton extent, merely for the pleasure of *destroying*, generally without stopping to cut out the meat". Chief Shoo-de-ga-cha of the Sioux told Catlin that his tribe

> had once been powerful and happy; that the buffalos which the Great Spirit had given them for food, and which formerly spread all over their green prairies, had all been killed or driven out

56 Indians used manufactured beads, brought into their country by the settlers, to decorate clothes and moccasins like these.

by the approach of white men, who wanted their skins; that their country was now entirely destitute of game, and even of roots for their food . . . .

All this became much worse in the 1860s and 1870s when the railways brought hunters out from the towns to enjoy a few days' sport. There was also a new demand for buffalo hides and for buffalo bones as fertilizer. By the 1880s Chief Sitting Bull said:

A cold wind blew across the prairie when the last buffalo fell . . . a death wind for my people.

Reservations

The Indians, who thought that the land was free for everyone, were slowly driven from their homelands. It was a gradual process. After the British defeat in the American War of Independence, Thomas Jefferson bought Louisiana from the French. This meant that settlers could move into western America, causing the Iroquois to retreat into Canada and the Seminole to go towards the swamplands of Florida. Some tribes did not want to fight and tried to adapt to new ways. The Cherokee, for instance, adopted many European habits and even had their own written language and newspaper. The "Five Civilized Tribes" who tried to come to terms with settlers in the late eighteenth century were the Chocktaw, Creek, Chickasaw, Seminole and Cherokee, but even they were doomed. In 1830 Andrew Jackson's Removal Act decreed that Indians living on the east of the Mississippi must move out into new territories. Many followed what became known as "The Trail of Tears", but others remained to fight. Gradually the tribes which had survived were restricted to Reservations, usually far away from their original homelands.

57 A Crow tribe Reservation, Montana, in about 1900. Tepees are mixed with government-issue tents.

The Indian wars

The Indian wars of the nineteenth century, familiar from Hollywood Westerns, were a last ditch stand by tribesmen who could not understand or want the new way of life. They were no match for the modern world, although many of the chiefs put up a spirited fight for their very existence. Indian children living in the period between 1840 and 1900 on the Great Plains must often have led miserable and frightened lives. Most of the time they would have been hungry and scared. The Cheyenne, for instance, who agreed to move into a Reservation in 1861, found that there was not enough food there for them to live on. They stole cattle in order to survive and were punished for this by the US Army,

58 A Sioux Reservation, Dakota, in the 1880s.
The tent and utensils were issued by the government.

under the command of Colonel John Chivington, whose opinion was, "Damn any man who sympathises with Indians. I have come to kill Indians, and believe it is right and honourable to use any means under God's heaven to kill Indians."

There was cruelty on both sides. Cowboys came into contact with marauding Indians when they were taking cattle to the trading posts and railheads. Immigrants were sometimes attacked and killed or taken prisoner. Tribes like the Sioux and Arapaho bitterly opposed the railway, which they called the "Iron Horse" and attacked the workmen on many occasions. In 1867 one Union

Pacific worker called William Thompson was scalped by the Cheyenne and carefully carried his scalp back to civilization in the vain hope that it could be fixed on again. Soldiers were appalled when they saw the mutilated bodies of friends who had been attacked by Indians. They also found it difficult to deal with Indian guerilla tactics, as they never knew whether civilians were hiding the fighters.

Many great Indian chiefs led their tribes in the fight for survival during the nineteenth century. They were courageous in battle and went into captivity with dignity, earning the respect of their enemies, if not their understanding. The Indians themselves were never able to understand the American attitude to land. They did not know why anyone should want to enclose the open prairies and forest and punish men for going there. They rightly saw no reason why they should be moved away from their homes to make way for white settlers. After the "Five Civilized Tribes" of the South East had been moved into Oklahoma, Osceola, chief of the Seminole, held out in the swamps of Florida for some years. He was finally captured by a trick in 1830 and taken to prison, where he died three

59 Cheyenne Indians destroy the Union Pacific railway line in 1869.

months later. The Nez Perce of the Plateau area were forced to leave their territory and move into a Reservation in 1877. Although the Indians agreed to this move, to avoid bloodshed, they were angered when some of their horses were stolen by the new settlers, and they fought back under their leader, Chief Joseph. They were no match for American soldiers and were forced to move back into Canada. They were attacked in the Bear Paw Mountains, and Chief Joseph surrendered in 1877, saying:

> My people ask me for food and I have none to give. It is cold and we have no blankets, no wood. My people are starving to death. Where is my little daughter? I do not know. Perhaps even now she is freezing to death. Hear me my chiefs, I have fought, but from where the sun now stands Joseph will fight no more forever.

In the south the Apache were feared by Americans and Mexicans. They were skilled at guerilla warfare and were bloodthirsty fighters. Although, theoretically, peace had been made with the various Apache bands by 1875, fierce fighting broke out again in 1882, under the Apache leader Geronimo. American newspapers were full of stories about the exploits of Geronimo and his band. After his capture Geronimo and his tribe were settled far from their native territory, in Oklahoma.

Sitting Bull, head of the Hunkpapa section of the Sioux, was one of the most famous Indian chiefs of the period. Gold was discovered in the tribal lands in 1874. Sitting Bull and another leader, Crazy Horse, refused to sell out and were attacked at Little Big Horn by Colonel Custer and the 7th Cavalry on 5 July 1876. Custer was killed with 260 of his soldiers. The end of

61   Chief Joseph of the Nez Perce.

the story came in 1890, when Sitting Bull and members of his tribe were massacred by the 7th Cavalry at the Battle of Wounded Knee. Innocent women and children were killed, and no one will ever know exactly why the army attacked. Fear of the Indians had been aggravated during this period by a revival of the Ghost Dance, which was believed to be a war dance. Some said afterwards that they had seen braves putting on their ghost shirts and dancing as a prelude to attack. After the battle, one of the female survivors, Louise Weasel Bear said:

CHIEF GERONIMO
APACHE

COPYRIGHT 1898
F.A. RINEHART.
OMAHA

66

They shot us like we were buffalo. I know there are some good white people, but the soldiers must be mean to shoot children and women.

By the end of the nineteenth century the Indian fight for survival was over. Today Indians live on Reservations or have merged into American society. Life on a Reservation little resembles the nomadic life of their forefathers. Children go to school like any

63 Navajo Indians pass through the majestic landscape of their homeland.

other American citizens. Indians are encouraged to produce the beautiful craftwork for which they are famous. Perhaps one can be closer to the Indians of the past in the natural landscape where they once lived. Many of the old territories have now become National Parks, and the wild, majestic scenery can give a more real understanding of the tribes that once wandered there at will.

◄ 62 Geronimo.

Date List

1492	Columbus discovers America
1519	Cortes and Spanish soldiers land in Mexico
1532	Pizarro and Spanish soldiers enter Peru
1584	Jacques Cartier's French expedition to Canada
1585	Sir Walter Raleigh's expedition lands in Virginia
1587	John White's expedition to Florida
1606	Founding of Jamestown. Captain John Smith, Powhatan & Pocahontas
1630	Founding of the Iroquois Confederacy
1776-83	American War of Independence
1803	Louisiana Purchase
1831-4	Chocktaw and Chickasaw moved to new Territories
1832	The Removal Bill.
	George Catlin sets out to record customs of North American Indians
1835	Capture of Osceola and defeat of Seminole resistance
1838 on	Cherokee take the "Trail of Tears"
1849	Gold discovered in California
1851-56	American Civil War
1861-71	Apache under Cochise take the warpath
1876	Battle of Little Big Horn and death of Custer
1877	Chief Joseph of the Nez Perce surrenders
1880s	Apache, under Geronimo, rebel again
1890	Battle of Wounded Knee
	Death of Chief Sitting Bull of the Hunkpapa Sioux

Glossary

adobe	mud used as cement or for bricks to build Pueblo houses
awl	small pointed stone for pricking leather
buckskin	cured, softened leather
calumet	tobacco pipe used as pipe of peace
coons	racoons
coup	touching an enemy with the hand or with a special coup stick
coyote	prairie wolf
cradleboard	wooden board used as baby's cradle
false face	Iroquois ceremonial mask
hogan	earth house used by Navajo
igloo	Eskimo house built of ice and snow
kachina	a spirit half-way between gods and men
lodge	house. Also used for secret society
longhouse	wooden house where several Indian families lived
maize	sweet corn
medicine	mystery, magic
Medicine Man	witch doctor, priest, shaman, magician
moccasin	soft shoe made of deerskin
parflèche	decorated leather carrying bag
pemmican	preserved meat or fish
Reservations	land allocated to Indians after they were removed from their homelands
scalping	cutting off skin and hair from the crown of the head
tepee	Tipi; tent-like home of Plains Indians
tomahawk	war axe with head of horn, stone or iron
totem pole	pole carved with animal emblems
travois	carrying sledge made from two tepee poles, tied with ropes and drawn by horses or dogs
wampum	shells or beads used as money and for decoration
wickieup	dome-shaped buildings made from branches and thatch
wigwam	building with rounded roof covered with woven mats or bark. See also wickieup

Books for Further Reading

Bell, W.A., *Redman & Buffalo*, 1868

Borland, Hal, *Where the Legends Die*, Puffin

Brandon, William, *American Heritage Book of Indians*, Eyre & Spottiswoode, 1968

Brown, Dee, *Bury My Heart at Wounded Knee*, Pan, 1973

Catlin, George, *Letters on North American Indians*, 1841

Gibson, Michael, *The American Indian*, Wayland, 1974

Grey Owl, *Pilgrims of the Wild*, Puffin

Jackdaw Publications, *Indians of North America*, Marigold Coleman, 1976; *Indians of Canada*, Edward Rogers, 1969

La Farge, Oliver, *The American Indian*, Golden Press, New York, 1960

Parker, Arthur C., *The Indian How Book*, Dover Publications, 1927/1973

Time Life Books, The "Old West" series, in particular *The Indians*

Ulyatt, Kenneth, *The Time of the Indian*, Kestral, 1975

Warner, John Anson, *The Life and Art of the North American Indian*, Hamlyn, 1975

White, Jon Manchip, *Everyday Life of the North American Indian*, Batsford, 1979

Index

The numbers in **bold type** refer to the figure numbers of the illustrations